The European Union

Political, Social, and Economic Cooperation

THE
EUROPEAN UNION

POLITICAL, SOCIAL, AND ECONOMIC COOPERATION

ESTONIA

by
Autumn Libal

Mason Crest Publishers
Philadelphia

Mason Crest Publishers Inc.
370 Reed Road, Broomall, Pennsylvania 19008
(866) MCP-BOOK (toll free)
www.masoncrest.com

First printing
1 2 3 4 5 6 7 8 9 10

Library of Congress Cataloging-in-Publication Data

Libal, Autumn.
  Estonia / by Autumn Libal.
      p. cm.—(The European Union : political, social, and economic cooperation)
  Includes bibliographical references and index.
    ISBN 1-4222-0044-2
    ISBN 1-4222-0038-8 (series)
  1. Estonia—Juvenile literature. 2. European Union—Estonia—Juvenile literature. I. Title. II. European Union (Series) (Philadelphia, Pa.)
  DK503.23.L53 2006
  947.98—dc22
                                    2005019666

Produced by Harding House Publishing Service, Inc.
www.hardinghousepages.com
Design by Benjamin Stewart.
Cover design by MK Bassett-Harvey.
Printed in the Hashemite Kingdom of Jordan.

CONTENTS

ESTONIA

European Union Member since 2004

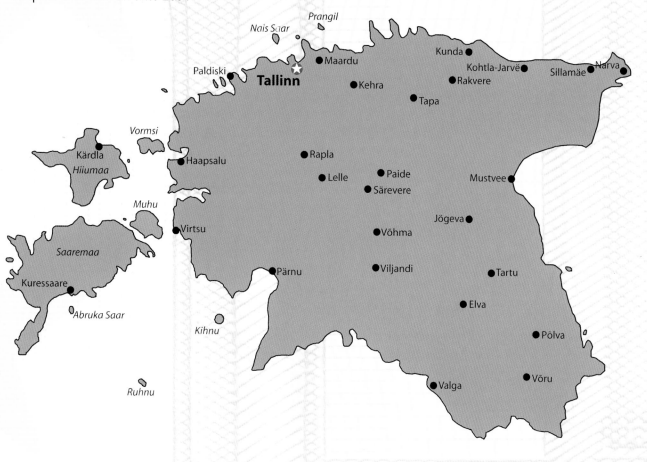

Nais Saar

Prangil

Paldiski

Maardu

Kunda

Kohtla-Jarvë

Sillamäe

Narva

Tallinn

Kehra

Rakvere

Tapa

Vormsi

Kärdla

Hiiumaa

Haapsalu

Rapla

Lelle

Paide

Mustvee

Muhu

Särevere

Virtsu

Jõgeva

Saaremaa

Võhma

Kuressaare

Pärnu

Viljandi

Tartu

Abruka Saar

Elva

Kihnu

Pölva

Ruhnu

Valga

Võru

INTRODUCTION

Sixty years ago, Europe lay scarred from the battles of the Second World War. During the next several years, a plan began to take shape that would unite the countries of the European continent so that future wars would be inconceivable. On May 9, 1950, French Foreign Minister Robert Schuman issued a declaration calling on France, Germany, and other European countries to pool together their coal and steel production as "the first concrete foundation of a European federation." "Europe Day" is celebrated each year on May 9 to commemorate the beginning of the European Union (EU).

The EU consists of twenty-five countries, spanning the continent from Ireland in the west to the border of Russia in the east. Eight of the ten most recently admitted EU member states are former communist regimes that were behind the Iron Curtain for most of the latter half of the twentieth century.

Any European country with a democratic government, a functioning market economy, respect for fundamental rights, and a government capable of implementing EU laws and policies may apply for membership. Bulgaria and Romania are set to join the EU in 2007. Croatia and Turkey have also embarked on the road to EU membership.

While the EU began as an idea to ensure peace in Europe through interconnected economies, it has evolved into so much more today:

- Citizens can travel freely throughout most of the EU without carrying a passport and without stopping for border checks.

- EU citizens can live, work, study, and retire in another EU country if they wish.

- The euro, the single currency accepted throughout twelve of the EU countries (with more to come), is one of the EU's most tangible achievements, facilitating commerce and making possible a single financial market that benefits both individuals and businesses.

- The EU ensures cooperation in the fight against cross-border crime and terrorism.

- The EU is spearheading world efforts to preserve the environment.

- As the world's largest trading bloc, the EU uses its influence to promote fair rules for world trade, ensuring that globalization also benefits the poorest countries.

- The EU is already the world's largest donor of humanitarian aid and development assistance, providing 55 percent of global official development assistance to developing countries in 2004.

The EU is neither a nation intended to replace existing nations, nor an international organization. The EU is unique—its member countries have established common institutions to which they delegate some of their sovereignty so that decisions on matters of joint interest can be made democratically at the European level.

Europe is a continent with many different traditions and languages, but with shared values such as democracy, freedom, and social justice, cherished values well known to North Americans. Indeed, the EU motto is "United in Diversity."

Enjoy your reading. Take advantage of this chance to learn more about Europe and the EU!

Ambassador John Bruton,
Head of Delegation of the European Commission, Washington, D.C.

While its northern climate presents special challenges for agriculture, Estonia's landscape includes many small farms.

1 THE LANDSCAPE

Part of the Baltic region of Eastern Europe, Estonia is a land kissed by the sea. The Gulf of Riga forms Estonia's western border, and the Baltic Sea and Gulf of Finland form its border to the north. Lake Peipsi laps the eastern shores. Estonia's only land borders are with Latvia to the south and a tiny boundary shared with Russia to the southeast. With an area of approximately 17,460 square miles (45,226 square kilometers), Estonia is a small country—roughly the size of Vermont and New Hampshire combined. In fact, it would only take a few hours to cross Estonia by car in any direction. Most of the country is mainland, but Estonia also lays claim to 1,521 islands that lie off its shores. These islands make up approximately one-tenth of Estonia's total landmass. The islands and Estonia's northern section are often referred to as Lower Estonia, while the central and southern regions are often called Upper Estonia.

A MARITIME CLIMATE

Estonia has a maritime climate, meaning its climate is moderated by the sea. Air masses over the Atlantic and the Baltic take on the water's temperature, then carry that temperature over the land. This results in cool summers and mild winters. Summer temperatures typically remain in the low 60s Fahrenheit (the high teens Celsius), while winter temperatures hover in the low 40s Fahrenheit (the mid-single digits Celsius). These averages are punctuated by warmer highs and colder lows, especially in the interior where temperatures are more extreme. For the most part, however, Estonia's climate is mild.

Estonia's record high:
97.7° Fahrenheit (36.5° Celsius), recorded in 1992

Estonia's record low:
−45.4° Fahrenheit (−41° Celsius), recorded in 1940

Its location on the sea results not only in cool temperatures, but also in cloudy skies, breezy weather, and frequent rain, especially in the spring and autumn months. In these months, the ocean winds often develop into storms. Estonia's western coast is called the "shore of winds" in honor of the storms that develop there. Much of Estonia receives snow in the winter. Depending on where you are in the country, however, the snow may not stick around for long because the mild weather results in repeated thaws.

MARSHLANDS, LAKES, FORESTS, AND MEADOWS

Stretching out from the sea, Estonia's land is largely flat and boggy. Marshland covers approximately one-fifth of this low-lying country, and much of the marshland is made up of peat bogs. The most impressive of these bogs can have peat twenty-three feet (7 meters) thick. The highest concentrations of marshland are in Estonia's central and eastern regions. Large sections of marshland have been drained to create farmland for raising crops and pasturing livestock. Wetlands are an important part of the water cycle. They are the earth's water-treatment facilities, filtering water as it

Much of central Estonia is flat, but the southeastern section of the country contains miles of small rolling hills.

drains through the marshes. Draining marshland is a common practice throughout the world, a practice that provides land for farming and development. But this practice also has many negative environmental consequences, including increasing water pollution and reducing animal habitat.

In some areas, Estonia's marshlands widen out to become lakes. The country is home to more than 1,400 lakes, the majority of which are located in the southern regions, where some hills roll across the landscape. Estonia's largest lake is Lake Peipsi, which the country shares with its eastern

QUICK FACTS: THE GEOGRAPHY OF ESTONIA

Location: Eastern Europe, bordering the Baltic Sea and the Gulf of Finland, between Latvia and Russia

Area: Slightly smaller than New Hampshire and Vermont combined*
  total: 17,462 square miles (45,226 sq. km.)
  land: 16,684 square miles (43,211 sq. km.)
  water: 778 square miles (2,015 sq. km.)

Borders: Latvia 211 miles (339 km.), Russia 183 miles (294 km.)

Climate: maritime, wet, moderate winters, cool summers

Terrain: marshy, lowlands, flat in the north, hilly in the south

Elevation extremes:
  lowest point: Baltic Sea 0 feet (0 meters)
  highest point: Suur Munamagi 1,043 feet (318 meters)

Natural hazards: occasional spring flooding

*Includes 1,520 small islands in the Baltic Sea.
Source: www.cia.org, 2005.

neighbor, Russia. Lake Peipsi is the fourth-largest lake in Europe. Nevertheless, it is surprisingly shallow, having an average depth of only twenty-three feet (7 meters) and a maximum depth of merely forty-nine feet (15 meters). Partly because it is so shallow, the lake is abundant with minerals and plant life. Draining into the lake are 237 rivers and streams from its roughly 17,000-square mile (44,200-square kilometer) **watershed**. About one million migratory birds call Lake Peipsi home for some part of the year, many of them feeding on the lake's bounty of fish and using its shores for nesting grounds. Lake Peipsi's natural fish stocks, as well as its fish farms, also make it an important part of Europe's commercial fishing industry. However, heavy industry carried out on its shores has caused great environmental damage to the lake. Overfishing, agricultural runoff, and untreated wastewater also threaten the lake's **sustainability**.

Throughout the country, Estonia's plentiful marshlands and lakes give way to forests. In fact, roughly half of Estonia is wooded, making it one of the most highly forested countries in the world. Few countries have such a large percentage of forested area remaining in their borders, and laws that limit development and **exploitation** of resources now protect much of Estonia's wooded land.

Estonia is also rich in meadowland, the most unique of which are its wooded meadows. Wooded meadows are a special type of meadowland that consists of sparsely dispersed tree stands and regularly mown vegetation. These meadows, though mown regularly, consist only of naturally growing plant species; the grasses are not sown by humans. Historically, wooded meadows were used largely to make hay for cattle. Once areas of rich **biodiversity**, almost all of Europe's wooded meadows have succumbed to the pressures of the

Moisture-laden winds sweep off the Baltic Sea, delivering enough rainfall for lush forests to grow in much of the country.

Estonia has more than 1,400 lakes, many of which are in the southern section of the country.

modern world. **Urbanization** and a movement away from small, family farms to large-scale agriculture have helped destroy wooded meadows and other natural landscapes in the rest of Europe. Estonia alone has managed to conserve some of these unique meadowlands, but here, too, the meadows are disappearing, taken over by new farming methods or simply abandoned by younger generations. The majority of Estonia's remaining wooded meadows are located in the western portion of the country. *Vahenurme* is the best preserved, boasting an incredible seventy-four plant species per square meter.

GEOLOGICAL FEATURES

One of Estonia's most stunning natural features is its limestone cliffs. They are part of a larger geological structure called the Baltic Glint, a huge wall of limestone that runs along the coast from Sweden all the way to Russia. Large sections of the Glint are under water, but in Estonia these sheer cliffs rise a majestic 160 feet (50 meters) from the water's surface toward the sky.

Estonia is also famous for the *Kaali* craters, which are located on *Saaremaa*, Estonia's largest island. The largest crater is 361 feet (110 meters) wide and 72 feet (22 meters) deep, making it the eighth-largest crater in the world. This, and eight smaller craters surrounding it, formed when a meteor broke apart and crashed to earth, probably about 7,500 years ago. Lake Kaali lies inside the largest crater. Also known as Holy Lake, Lake Kaali served as a site for animal sacrifices and other religious offerings for centuries.

Estonia's *Suur Munamagi* (Great Egg Hill) is the highest point in the Baltic region. It rises 1,043 feet (318 meters) above sea level, a great height for these otherwise flat coastal lands.

ESTONIA'S FLORA AND FAUNA

When it comes to flora, or plant life, Estonia is in many ways a transitional region. Hundreds of plant species, including the Siberian iris, ivy, and the Arctic bramble, reach the limits of their habit within Estonia's borders. There are also some plants, such as the Saaremaa yellow rattle and the Estonian saw wart, that cannot be found anywhere else in the world. The island of Saaremaa is also home to rare orchids. The country as a whole boasts a total of 1,538 species and subspecies of **vascular** plants, 2,500 species of algae, 680 species of **lichen**, and about 4,500 species of fungi. About sixty of Estonia's mushroom species are edible.

For such a small country, Estonia also has a surprising variety of forest types. Fresh boreo-nemoral forests, fresh boreal forests, dry boreal forests, boreal heath forests, minerotrophic mobile water swamp forests, and ombrotrophic bog forests can all be found within the country's borders. Rich soil, a mixture of spruce and broad-leaved trees like oak and maple, and thick undergrowth characterize fresh boreo-nemoral forests. In fresh boreal forests, spruce is dominant, undergrowth is thinner, and the soil, though still rich, is not as fertile as that of the fresh boreo-nemoral forest. The soil of the dry boreal forest is poorer still. These are pine forests with undergrowth made up

Estonia's marshes and bogs are a valuable habitat for endangered birds and other wildlife.

EUROPEAN UNION—ESTONIA

mostly of mosses and small plants. They are subject to forest fires, which are a natural part of the dry boreal forest's life cycle. Boreal heath forests have nutrient-poor, sandy soils, stunted pine trees, and undergrowth made up mostly of lichens. Minerotrophic mobile water swamp forests are located in valleys and floodplains. Black alder is the main species of tree found in these forests, and various water-loving plants, such as the marsh marigold and the bog arum, form the undergrowth. Ombrotrophic bog forests are floating pine forests. Here, the greatly stunted pines and other shrubs and plants grow from the **peat** that floats in the bog.

Estonia is also rich in fauna, or animal life. Located within the East Atlantic flyway, a migratory route between northeastern Europe and the arctic, Estonia's skies are graced with hundreds of bird species. A number of eagle types, including the golden eagle, white-tailed eagle, and the exceedingly rare spotted eagle, nest in Estonia. Barnacle geese, mute swans, white storks, and loons are among the birds that call the country home for at least part of the year. Estonia's islands and marshlands make excellent breeding grounds for many of these seasonal visitors.

Estonia's Baltic islands are also prime habitat for a number of seal species. They are just a few of the sixty-four species of mammals that inhabit the country. The European otter is far more common in Estonia than in other European nations. The brown bear, wolf, and lynx have also managed to survive within this country's borders. Other mammals, however, such as the flying squir-

The rocky soil of Estonia presents its own challenges, but the natives have farmed sections of the land for centuries.

rel, have become extremely rare, and some, like the European mink, are now believed to be extinct. Only five species of reptiles—three lizard species and two snake species—live in Estonia.

It is not just Estonia's land that supports fauna, but also Estonia's waters. The country's gulfs, rivers, and lakes are home to sixty-five fish species and eleven amphibians. But Estonia's entire population of mammals, birds, reptiles, fish, and amphibians cannot even begin to compare to its population of insects and other **invertebrates**, of which there are more than 18,500 species inhabiting its land and waters.

No longer a quiet Baltic city, Tallinn now has a night-life that keeps the streets filled until late in the evening.

2 CHAPTER

ESTONIA'S HISTORY AND GOVERNMENT

The land that is now Estonia has had permanent human settlements longer than almost any other area of Europe. ***Archaeological*** evidence suggests that humans have been living in the Baltic region for between nine thousand and eleven thousand years. Prior to this time, the earth experienced the Great Ice Age, and the

Historical re-creations seem perfectly apropos in the wonderfully preserved city of Tallinn.

Baltic region was covered by glaciers, making it unfit for human habitation. As the ice retreated, Estonia's first human inhabitants began moving in. These first settlers lived in small tribes and hunted and fished for survival.

FROM THE FINNO-UGRIC TRIBES TO THE SWEDISH ERA

Over the centuries, some of the tribal peoples adopted agrarian lifestyles—they supported them-

selves through the agricultural practices of crop and animal raising. This led to more permanent settlements. Trade with other parts of Europe also developed as the many water bodies around Estonia made ideal trade routes. By the thirteenth century, Estonia had a population of roughly 100,000 people. Society was loosely organized, and Estonia as a **nation-state** still did not exist.

The native Estonian people were of Finno-Ugric heritage, meaning that they spoke languages from the Uralic language family rather than the Indo-European languages that were spoken in most of Europe. They practiced **pagan** religions, and were some of the last pagan populations in Europe when they were finally converted to Christianity by the Christian **Crusades** of the thirteenth century.

In the early part of the thirteenth century, life in the Baltic region began to change as armies advanced from other parts of Europe. German, Danish, Swedish, and Russian conquerors descended on Estonia and divided it into **feudal** states. The first towns were established, and the conquerors' religions—first Roman

Catholicism and later Lutheranism—began to be adopted. The people had to pay taxes to their feudal overlords, and in the following centuries, debt forced the peasant population into **serfdom**. In the late 1600s and early 1700s, the Livonian War, famine, and a plague **decimated** the Estonian people. But by the mid-seventeenth century, Swedish rulers controlled the Estonian territory, and life improved. The Swedish Era, or "the good old Swedish time," as it is sometimes called, lasted for almost one hundred years. But in 1710, Russian aggression brought the region back under Russian control through a brutal war that ravaged the native population once again.

FROM THE RUSSIAN ERA TO INDEPENDENCE

In 1721, Estonia officially became part of Russia and would remain so until 1918. Despite attempts to **supplant** the native culture with Russian culture—a process called Russification—native Estonians began to see themselves as having a national identity separate from that of their overlords. Some peasants **advocated** for change, and eventually serfdom was lifted. Education among native Estonians increased, and between the 1860s and the 1880s, the Estonians experienced a period known as the Era of Enlightenment or the National Awakening. This movement promoted Estonian language and culture through publications, research, cultural organizations, the establishment of a national theater, and other advancements.

Estonia played an important role in the Russian Revolution, which began in 1905. In 1918, Estonia declared its independence from Russia, and its War of Liberation began. The Estonian Armed Forces fought against both Russian and German armies until the war's end in 1920.

Estonia's first taste of independence was short lived. During the Russian Revolution, Russia's **tsar** was overthrown and a new, **communist** government was established. In 1939, barely twenty years after independence was declared, the Soviet army began establishing military bases in Estonia—a sure sign the Soviet Union wanted to extend its control over the Baltic land.

FROM THE SOVIET ERA TO INDEPENDENCE AGAIN

Ultimately, Soviet occupation of Estonia came about through political dealings between Stalin and Hitler. In secret negotiations, these power-hungry leaders carved up Eastern Europe between Soviet Russia and Nazi Germany in what was called the Molotov-Ribbentrop Pact. Estonia, caught between two powerful neighbors, became a pawn in Soviet Russia's and Nazi Germany's expansionist plans and fell into the Soviet sphere of power. The immediate aftermath of Soviet occupation were tens of thousands of deaths and deportations as the Soviet Union attempted to purge the country of people it considered undesirable.

As World War II gained intensity, the German-Russian nonaggression pact was violated. Germans advanced along the eastern frontier into Russia itself. Germany rolled through Estonia, seizing it from Soviet hands and exacting near total destruction on the country's Jewish population and a terrible toll on many other Estonians.

The Second World War ended in Europe with the defeat of Nazi Germany. The Soviet Union reestablished itself in much of Eastern Europe, including Estonia. The communist system was exported from Russia to Estonia. As a result, farms were **collectivized** and industrialization began. Politically, the population found its freedoms restricted.

The Soviet Union fell apart in 1991 when a dramatic **coup** resulted in the overthrow and dissolution of the communist party. One after another, the satellite states declared their independence from Russia. Estonia was no exception. It declared its sovereignty, drafted a new constitution, and in 1992 held elections to form the new government.

ESTONIA'S GOVERNMENT TODAY

Today Estonia is a parliamentary republic, which means that the government is controlled by the people (in this case through their elected representatives) rather than by a monarch, dictator, military, or other supreme leader or body. In Estonia, all citizens age eighteen and older have the right to vote.

The Alexander Nevsky Cathedral, pictured at left, was built in the 1890s
and is testament to Russia's efforts to impose its culture on the area.

The view from the "upper town" of Old Tallinn shows the mix of historical architecture.
The nearby Tallinn Bay is visible in the background.

Estonia's parliament is called the *Riigikogu*, which means National Council. It consists of 101 officials who are democratically elected by the Estonian people. The parliament elects the president, and the president appoints a prime minister. Parliamentary elections are held every four years. The president's term lasts for five years and the president can serve a maximum of two terms. To be elected president, a candidate must receive a two-thirds majority in the parliamentary voting. If, however, the two-thirds majority cannot be reached in three rounds of voting, an electoral assembly will be formed from parliament and local government officials. The electoral assembly chooses a president from the two most popular candidates.

Estonia's capital is the city of Tallinn. The country is divided into fifteen counties from which leaders are elected. There are currently eight political parties. The Center Party is the most powerful, taking up one-quarter of the seats in parliament. The Social Democratic Party, with only six parliamentarians, is the least powerful political party.

Tartu, the cradle of 19th century Estonian nationalism, was devastated by World War II but now has been rebuilt and is a national center for technological development and research.

3 CHAPTER

THE ECONOMY

Economically, Estonia is one of the most successful of the former Soviet states. After the Soviet Union's fall, Estonia enthusiastically embraced capitalism. Today Estonia can truly be called a land of free trade, for it has extremely liberal trade laws with almost no customs tariffs, no corporate tax, and very few limitations on foreign investment. These conditions have attracted businesses and investors from abroad and have helped the Estonian currency, the kroon (EEK) maintain stability. Throughout the 1990s, many other former Soviet states saw their monetary systems fall into rapid decline and their currencies lose value. Today, the kroon is pegged to the euro, meaning that its value rises and falls at the

Estonia's gross domestic product (GDP), or the value of all the goods and services produced within the country in a given year, is approximately $19.23 billion. Divided by the population, that would average out to about $14,300 per person. The average amount of money per person is called the per capita GDP, and Estonia's is the highest among the Baltic States.

Estonia's relatively high GDP does not mean that in reality this wealth is distributed equally. In fact, nearly 30 percent of the country's wealth is concentrated in the upper-most 10 percent of the population; the lowest 10 percent of the population has only 3 percent of the country's wealth. Furthermore, approximately one-third of the population lives below the poverty line, and nearly 80 percent of the country's wealth is concentrated within Tallinn's capital region.

QUICK FACTS: THE ECONOMY OF ESTONIA

Gross Domestic Product (GDP): US$19.23 billion
GDP per capita: US$14,300
Industries: engineering, electronics, wood and wood products, textiles, information technology, telecommunications
Agriculture: potatoes, vegetables; livestock and dairy products; fish
Export commodities: machinery and equipment, wood and paper, textiles, food products, furniture, metals, chemical products (2001)
Export partners: Finland 16.6%, Sweden 11.1%, UK 8.6%, Latvia 7.4%, Germany 7.2%, Russia 6.9%, U.S. 5.5%, Lithuania, 4%
Import commodities: machinery and equipment, chemical products, textiles, foodstuffs, transportation equipment 8.9% (2001)
Import partners: Finland 19.9%, Russia 13.2%, Germany 11.6%, Sweden 7.9%
Currency: Estonian kroon (EEK)
Currency exchange rate: US$1 = 13.13 EEK (July 6, 2005)

Note: All figures are from 2004 unless otherwise noted.
Source: www.cia.org, 2005.

same rate as the euro. One American dollar is worth about thirteen kroon. Estonia's stable economy was a major factor in its admittance to the European Union (EU). Estonia is also a member of the World Trade Organization.

At 9.6 percent, Estonia's unemployment rate is quite high.

In 2004, Estonia's GDP grew by 6 percent, and the inflation rate was 3 percent. The country ran on a balanced budget, with revenues of approximate-

Estonia's service sector, including banking, accounts for 67 percent of Estonia's gross domestic product.

ly $4.6 billion and a nearly equal amount of expenditures. Despite the balanced budget, the country still has a relatively high debt; nearly $8.4 billion is owed outside the country. Estonia received $108 million in economic aid in 2000.

AGRICULTURE, INDUSTRY, AND SERVICES

Estonia's economy can be divided into three categories: agriculture, industry, and services.

Amber, which now fills gift shops throughout Estonia, used to be one of the primary products traded in the Baltic area.

Estonians were once an almost exclusively agricultural people. Today, however, agriculture makes up a very small portion of the overall economy, accounting for only 4.1 percent of the GDP. The main agricultural products are potatoes, vegetables, livestock, dairy products, and fish.

The Soviet Union always placed a huge emphasis on industry, and industry grew in Estonia during Soviet times. Today industry continues to make up 28.9 percent of the GDP. The main industries are engineering, electronics, wood and wood products, textiles, information technology, and telecommunications.

The largest portion of the GDP, however, comes from Estonia's service sector. Services account for 67 percent of the country's wealth. Banking and finance make up a strong portion of the service sector. Estonia has also developed a healthy tourism industry.

EXPORTS, IMPORTS, AND TRADING PARTNERS

Estonia exports about $5.7 billion worth of goods each year. Exports consist mostly of machinery and equipment, wood and paper, and textiles, but food products, furniture, metals, and chemical products are also exported. Estonia's biggest trading partner is Finland. Sweden is also an extremely important trading partner. Smaller, but still important trading partners are the United Kingdom, Latvia, Germany, Russia, the United States, and Lithuania.

Estonia imports more goods than it exports, about $7.3 billion dollars worth per year. Interestingly, while machinery and equipment are the country's biggest export, they are also its biggest import. Chemical products are the next biggest import followed by textiles, foodstuffs, and transportation equipment. The largest amounts of imports come from Finland. Significant amounts of imports also come from Russia, Germany, and Sweden.

Estonians possess an appreciation of the fine arts, shown by the many examples of public art found in their parks.

4 Estonia's People and Culture

Like their ethnic cousins the Finns, the Estonian people are known for being reserved. A calm, quiet demeanor and good manners are respected, while rowdiness and uncouth behavior are highly frowned on. Estonians are a well-educated people; their literacy rate is 99.8 percent. The Estonian culture has also tended to be more Western leaning than in other ex-Soviet nations.

While the Lutheran Church dominates Estonian religious life,
other faiths from Hindu to Russian Orthodox are also represented within the nation.

This is largely due to the fact that, even during the communist era, Estonia maintained strong ties with Finland. Tourists and intellectuals from Finland brought Western ideas and culture to Estonia, and the northern third of the country was even able to access Western television broadcasts from Finland. These things helped smooth Estonia's transition when the Soviet Union fell.

ESTONIA'S POPULATION

Estonia has a population of approximately 1,332,900 people. Of these, however, only 67.9 percent are ethnic Estonians. The rest of Estonia's population has its roots in other lands. The largest group after ethnic Estonians is people of Russian descent; they make up 25.6 percent of the population. There are other significant ethnic populations including Ukrainians (2.1 percent), Belarusians (1.3 percent), and Finns (.9 percent). Although many of their groups may not be large enough to constitute a significant percentage of the population, people from about 120 nationalities live in Estonia.

Estonia has a declining population. This is due in large part to a very low birth rate and a relatively high death rate. There are only 9.91 births per 1,000 people each year, and there are 13.21 deaths per 1,000 people each year. The United States, in comparison, has 14.14 births and 8.25 deaths per 1,000 people each year. Estonia's total fertility rate is a low 1.39 children per woman. Another factor in Estonia's shrinking population is the net migration rate, or the total number of peo-

Quick Facts: The People of Estonia

Population: 1,332,893

Ethnic groups: Estonian 67.9%, Russian 25.6%, Ukranian 2.1%, Belarusian 1.3%, Finn 0.9%, other 2.2% (2000)

Age structure:
- *0–14 years:* 15.5%
- *15–64 years:* 67.7%
- *65 years and over:* 16.8%

Population growth rate: –0.65%

Birth rate: 9.91 births/1,000 pop.

Death rate: 13.21 deaths/1,000 pop.

Migration rate: –3.18 migrant(s)/1,000 pop.

Infant mortality rate: 7.87 deaths/1,000 live births

Life expectancy at birth:
- *Total population:* 71.77 years
- *Male:* 66.28 years
- *Female:* 77.60 years

Total fertility rate: 1.39 children born/woman

Religions: Evangelical Lutheran, Russian Orthodox, Estonian Orthodox, Baptist, Methodist, Seventh-Day Adventist, Roman Catholic, Pentecostal, Word of Life, Jewish (2000)

Languages: Estonian (official), Russian, Ukrainian, Finnish, other (2000)

Literacy rate: 99.8% (2003)

Note: All figures are from 2005 unless otherwise noted.
Source: www.cia.org, 2005.

migration rate of –3.18 migrants per 1,000 people.

Life expectancy rates in Estonia continue to be relatively low. The average life expectancy is 71.77 years. Men, however, have a much lower life expectancy than women: only 66.28 years compared to women's expected 77.6 years.

LANGUAGE

Language is somewhat of a touchy subject in Estonia. During Soviet times, Russian was the official language, and some Estonians still see the use of Russian as an affront to their culture and independence. Today, Estonian is the official language of the country, but many members of the country's large Russian population now feel that their culture is the one threatened. In fact, Estonia has some relatively strict laws governing the use of languages. For instance, anyone running for parliament or other public offices must be proficient in Estonian. In most cases, it is also illegal to display words in another language on billboards or shop windows. Some feel that these language laws, though meant to protect

ple a nation gains or loses through immigration to or emigration from the country. Estonia loses more people through emigration than it gains through immigration, resulting in an annual net

The old walls of Old Town Tallinn contain something for tourists and also young stunt bicycle riders.

The National Theater presents a stark modern contrast to the nearby medieval architecture in Tallinn's Old Town.

Estonian culture and integrate smaller ethnic groups into the larger whole, actually serve to isolate other language groups. Many Russians, for example, still do not speak Estonian, and language laws barring those who don't speak proficient Estonian from holding public office limit the Russian population's political participation and representation.

RELIGION

Religious practice is less common in Estonia than it is in North America. In fact, in surveys, more Estonians claim no religious affiliation than claim to be religious. Russian-speaking Estonians tend to be more religious than ethnic Estonians. Among Estonians who do practice religion, many are Lutheran; they make up 13.6 percent of the population. Members of the Orthodox Church make up 12.8 percent of the population. Other Christian denominations, such as Seventh-Day Adventist and Roman Catholic, are also practiced, but they make up a very small percentage of the population, only 1.4 percent.

THE ARTS

The arts are very important for Estonians, who see the arts as a way to protect their culture and keep it alive. To this end, theater is a significant Estonian art. The first professional theater began in Estonia in 1906. The art form gained popularity quickly, and more theater houses opened. During Soviet occupation, Estonians clung to their theater as a symbol of cultural independence. Donations from private citizens funded the building of many of Estonia's theaters.

Theater is not the only art form close to Estonian hearts. Estonian classical music is taken very seriously at home and has gained international recognition. Choirs are especially well loved. Classical music, however, is far from the only musical form Estonians enjoy. All over Europe, dance and techno music pack droves of people (mostly young) into clubs and raves. Estonia is no exception, and dance music is as popular here as in the rest of Europe. Rock is also extremely popular with U.S., European, and local Estonian bands all having large fan bases.

Estonia's literary history is not a long one. An Estonian text may have been written in the 1500s, but writings by and available to people other than the clergy did not begin appearing until about 150 years ago. Despite its relatively short history, today Estonia's literary tradition is thriving, and Estonia has produced two Nobel Prize nominees. One is Jaan Kross, who during the Soviet era was exiled for a time in Siberia and now writes historical novels. The other is poet Jaan Kaplinski.

THE SETU AND THE RUSSIAN OLD BELIEVERS

The Setu and the Russian Old Believers are two of Estonia's ethnic minorities. The Setu live along Lake Peipsi's southern side. They speak a dialect of Estonian with strong Russian influences. For years, Estonia and Russia argued over their land border,

The Alexander Nevsky Cathedral, a symbol of Russian domination, is viewed with mixed feelings by Estonians.

and the Setu were caught in the middle. In 2005, the two countries finally came to an official agreement, and as a result the Setu area is divided by the Estonian-Russian border. The Estonian government has offered to help Setu living on the Russian side relocate their villages to the Estonian side, but this does not appease many Setu who wanted an old border agreement honored, which would have left the Setu area intact.

The Russian Old Believers live mostly along Lake Peipsi's western shore. Fleeing religious persecution, the first Old Believers came to Estonia in the late 1600s. They are called Old Believers because they refused to except reforms made to the Russian Orthodox Church in 1652. Today they continue their centuries-old religious traditions, and their community consists of roughly 15,000 members.

More than a full decade after Estonia broke free of the Soviet Union, the nation continues to transform itself. Old factories and warehouses are transformed or destroyed in the process.

5 CHAPTER THE CITIES

Of course it would be impossible to discuss all of Estonia's cities and towns here, but a brief overview of some of the largest and most notable shows the diversity of culture, language, history, and environment within which Estonians live.

TALLINN

Estonia's capital city, Tallinn, has a population of nearly 400,000 people, making it the country's largest city. It is a place where old and new mix, and in it one can find everything from medieval architecture to Internet cafes.

Tallinn is located on the Gulf of Finland. It is an important port city, and its location has significantly impacted its history. For centuries, Tallinn's position along the trade route between Russian lands and the west made it desirable, and the city has been controlled at various times by the Danish, Germans, Swedish, and Russians.

Today Tallinn and the surrounding area is the most prosperous part of Estonia. Tallinn's Old Town, with its **_impeccably_** preserved medieval turrets, fortress walls, and remains of a thirteenth-century castle, is surrounded by a thoroughly modern and bustling business district. Tallinn can also be called Estonia's most multicultural city. Forty percent of the city is Russian, and many of the city's residents speak multiple languages. Tallinn is a favorite destination for tourists, and some people say the city and its residents are culturally more Scandinavian than Eastern European. For this reason, the city is sometimes nicknamed Tallsinki.

NARVA

Located 130 miles (210 kilometers) west of Tallinn on Estonia's Russian border lies the city of Narva. The city has a population of roughly 68,000, approximately 96 percent of whom are Russian. In many ways, Narva's situation is a sad one. Soviet industry wreaked havoc on the area's environment and gave the city the infamous distinction of being one of the most polluted in Europe. Cleanup has been a priority, but also a massive task, and it may be overly optimistic to expect that any area so decimated will ever be able to adequately recover. Furthermore, rehabilitation efforts are hampered by the economic situation. The city has lost much of its industrial economic base and now boasts one of the highest unemployment rates in the country.

Narva has been an area of controversy for another reason. Only the Narva River separates Narva and its residents from the Russian city Ivangorod. In fact, viewing the area from above, one might think they are the same city. Many residents wish they were, and over the years since Estonian independence, there have been calls for Narva to be annexed to Russia or for Ivangorod to be annexed to Estonia. Almost surely neither will happen, and their border crossing will continue to be the busiest in all of Estonia.

EUROPEAN UNION—ESTONIA

The cobblestoned Town Hall Square is a central meeting place for residents and tourists alike.

Parnu is famous for its health promoting spas, such as the one pictured above. Many offer therapeutic mud treatments.

PÄRNU

Pärnu is located just eighty-one miles (130 kilometers) south of Tallinn. It has a population of roughly 45,500 people and a reputation for being a bit of a party town because of the tourists drawn to its sandy beaches. Pärnu is also a well-known place for relaxation and recuperation because of its many sanatoriums, places people go to for therapeutic treatments for physical or mental illnesses or disorders. This may make sanatoriums sound like hospitals, but in many cases they can be more like therapeutic spas, and thousands of people from the Baltic and Scandinavian region travel to Pärnu each year for some rest and relaxation. Pärnu is also gaining a reputation for its art galleries and museums.

TARTU

Located in the central, eastern portion of Estonia, Tartu is a happening college town with a traditional Estonian feel. It has approximately 101,100 residents and takes pride in the fact that it was less touched by the Soviet era's militarism and industrialization than other cities and areas of the country.

Estonia's first university was established in Tartu in 1632 (although at that time the area was under Swedish control), making the city not only the oldest university town in Estonia, but one of the oldest in all of Europe. At about the same time, the town also became the site of Estonia's first printing press. In 1775, Tartu was almost completely destroyed by a great fire, but was rebuilt, and the town's history as a preeminent Estonian community continued. In the next century, Estonia's first student/nationalist organizations formed in Tartu. In fact, the city was the center of Estonia's national awakening, and the university played a large role in **catalyzing** and **perpetuating** this movement. Today, the university students continue to influence culture in Tartu, encouraging academic debate and progressive thinking.

In addition to its educational emphasis, Tartu is also home to many cultural festivals and important sporting events. The annual Estonian Song Festivals often begin in Tartu. The Tartu Ski Marathon draws hundreds of skiers in February, and the Tartu Bicycle Marathon attracts cyclists in May and September. Theatre Vanemuine was Estonia's first professional theater, and it has three halls in Tartu: the Big House, the Small House, and the Port Theatre. With its many beautiful parks and surrounding areas, Tartu is also a city close to nature.

SILLAMÄE

Although most of Estonia has enthusiastically moved beyond the Soviet era, the town of Sillamäe is in some ways a living museum to this past. Though it is a small place, really a town rather than a city, it is noteworthy. It has a population of roughly 17,200 people, and of those, 94 percent are Russian. Their history in this town is a fascinating one, shrouded by the mystery that comes with once being a Soviet military secret.

ETTEVAATUST
VARINGUOHT!

BE CAUTIOUS!
THE BUILDING IS LIABLE
TO FALL DOWN!

The ruined Toomkirik, or dome church, dates from the thirteenth century. The structure stands next to Tartu's Museum of Books.

People have lived in the area of Sillamäe since the 1500s, but it was only during the Soviet era that the town was truly established and grew. The town's birth came from the search for nuclear fuel, and for years outsiders were barred entry and maps failed to show Sillamäe's name and location. Five thousand political prisoners and nearly four thousand prisoners of war were sent from Russia to Sillamäe (which at the time was first called Moscow 400, then Leningrad 1, and finally Narva 1) to build a uranium-processing factory and a town center.

Today the hulking factory buildings stand cold and empty, stern ghosts testifying to the town and the nation's past. Far more frightening, however, is what is out of sight: the nuclear waste the factory produced, now buried in a concrete grave by the sea. Estonia has been very successful in building a new economy and hopeful future, but there are some specters of the past from which it will never be free.

The EU flag

6 CHAPTER

THE FORMATION OF THE EUROPEAN UNION

The EU is an economic and political confederation of twenty-five European nations. Member countries abide by common foreign and security policies and cooperate on judicial and domestic affairs. The confederation, however, does not replace existing states or governments. Each of the twenty-five member states is **autonomous**, but they have all agreed to establish some common institutions and to hand over some of their own decision-making powers to these international bodies. As a result, decisions on matters that interest all member states can be made democratically, accommodating everyone's concerns and interests.

Today, the EU is the most powerful regional organization in the world. It has evolved from a primarily economic organization to an increasingly political one. Besides promoting economic cooperation, the EU requires that its members uphold fundamental values of peace and **solidarity**, human dignity, freedom, and equality. Based on the principles of democracy and the rule of law, the EU respects the culture and organizations of member states.

History

The seeds of the EU were planted more than fifty years ago in a Europe reduced to smoking piles of rubble by two world wars. European nations suffered great financial difficulties in the postwar period. They were struggling to get back on their feet and realized that another war would cause further hardship. Knowing that internal conflict was hurting all of Europe, a drive began toward European cooperation.

France took the first historic step. On May 9, 1950 (now celebrated as Europe Day), Robert Schuman, the French foreign minister, proposed the coal and steel industries of France and West Germany be coordinated under a single supranational authority. The proposal, known as the Treaty

of Paris, attracted four other countries—Belgium, Luxembourg, the Netherlands, and Italy—and resulted in the 1951 formation of the European Coal and Steel Community (ECSC). These six countries became the founding members of the EU.

In 1957, European cooperation took its next big leap. Under the Treaty of Rome, the European Economic Community (EEC) and the European Atomic Energy Community (EURATOM) were formed. Informally known as the Common Market, the EEC promoted joining the national economies into a single European economy. The 1965 Treaty of Brussels (more commonly referred to as the Merger Treaty) united these various treaty organizations under a single umbrella, the European Community (EC).

In 1992, the Maastricht Treaty (also known as the Treaty of the European Union) was signed in Maastricht, the Netherlands, signaling the birth of the EU as it stands today. **Ratified** the following year, the Maastricht Treaty provided for a central banking system, a common currency (the euro) to replace the national currencies, a legal definition of the EU, and a framework for expanding the

The EU's united economy has allowed it to become a worldwide financial power.

EU's political role, particularly in the area of foreign and security policy.

By 1993, the member countries completed their move toward a single market and agreed to participate in a larger common market, the European Economic Area, established in 1994.

The EU, headquartered in Brussels, Belgium, reached its current member strength in spurts. In

© BCE ECB EZB EKT EKP 2002

© BCE ECB EZB EKT EKP 2002

© BCE ECB EZB EKT EKP 2002

© BCE ECB EZB EKT EKP 2002

The euro, the EU's currency

1973, Denmark, Ireland, and the United Kingdom joined the six founding members of the EC. They were followed by Greece in 1981, and Portugal and Spain in 1986. The 1990s saw the unification of the two Germanys, and as a result, East Germany entered the EU fold. Austria, Finland, and Sweden joined the EU in 1995, bringing the total number of member states to fifteen. In 2004, the EU nearly doubled its size when ten countries—Cyprus, the Czech Republic, Estonia, Hungary, Latvia, Lithuania, Malta, Poland, Slovakia, and Slovenia—became members.

The EU Framework

The EU's structure has often been compared to a "roof of a temple with three columns." As established by the Maastricht Treaty, this three-pillar framework encompasses all the policy areas—or pillars—of European cooperation. The three pillars of the EU are the European Community, the Common Foreign and Security Policy (CFSP), and Police and Judicial Co-operation in Criminal Matters.

Quick Facts: The European Union

Number of Member Countries: 25
Official Languages: 20—Czech, Danish, Dutch, English, Estonian, Finnish, French, German, Greek, Hungarian, Italian, Latvian, Lithuanian, Maltese, Polish, Portuguese, Slovak, Slovenian, Spanish, and Swedish; additional language for treaty purposes: Irish Gaelic
Motto: *In Varietate Concordia* (United in Diversity)
European Council's President: Each member state takes a turn to lead the council's activities for 6 months.
European Commission's President: José Manuel Barroso (Portugal)
European Parliament's President: Josep Borrell (Spain)
Total Area: 1,502,966 square miles (3,892,685 sq. km.)
Population: 454,900,000
Population Density: 302.7 people/square mile (116.8 people/sq. km.)
GDP: €9.61.1012
Per Capita GDP: €21,125
Formation:
- Declared: February 7, 1992, with signing of the Maastricht Treaty
- Recognized: November 1, 1993, with the ratification of the Maastricht Treaty

Community Currency: Euro. Currently 12 of the 25 member states have adopted the euro as their currency.
Anthem: "Ode to Joy"
Flag: Blue background with 12 gold stars arranged in a circle
Official Day: Europe Day, May 9

Source: europa.eu.int

PILLAR ONE

The European Community pillar deals with economic, social, and environmental policies. It is a body consisting of the European Parliament, European Commission, European Court of Justice, Council of the European Union, and the European Courts of Auditors.

PILLAR TWO

The idea that the EU should speak with one voice in world affairs is as old as the European integration process itself. Toward this end, the Common Foreign and Security Policy (CFSP) was formed in 1993.

PILLAR THREE

The cooperation of EU member states in judicial and criminal matters ensures that its citizens enjoy the freedom to travel, work, and live securely and safely anywhere within the EU. The third pillar—Police and Judicial Co-operation in Criminal Matters—helps to protect EU citizens from international crime and to ensure equal access to justice and fundamental rights across the EU.

The flags of the EU's nations:

top row, left to right
Belgium, the Czech Republic, Denmark, Germany, Estonia, Greece

second row, left to right
Spain, France, Ireland, Italy, Cyprus, Latvia

third row, left to right
Lithuania, Luxembourg, Hungary, Malta, the Netherlands, Austria

bottom row, left to right
Poland, Portugal, Slovenia, Slovakia, Finland, Sweden, United Kingdom

ECONOMIC STATUS

As of May 2004, the EU had the largest economy in the world, followed closely by the United States. But even though the EU continues to enjoy a trade surplus, it faces the twin problems of high unemployment rates and **stagnancy**.

The 2004 addition of ten new member states is expected to boost economic growth. EU membership is likely to stimulate the economies of these relatively poor countries. In turn, their prosperity growth will be beneficial to the EU.

THE EURO

The EU's official currency is the euro, which came into circulation on January 1, 2002. The shift to the euro has been the largest monetary changeover in the world. Twelve countries—Belgium, Germany, Greece, Spain, France, Ireland, Italy, Luxembourg, the Netherlands, Finland, Portugal, and Austria—have adopted it as their currency.

SINGLE MARKET

Within the EU, laws of member states are harmonized and domestic policies are coordinated to create a larger, more-efficient single market.

The chief features of the EU's internal policy on the single market are:

- free trade of goods and services

- a common EU competition law that controls anticompetitive activities of companies and member states

- removal of internal border control and harmonization of external controls between member states

- freedom for citizens to live and work anywhere in the EU as long as they are not dependent on the state

- free movement of **capital** between member states

- harmonization of government regulations, corporation law, and trademark registration

- a single currency

- coordination of environmental policy

- a common agricultural policy and a common fisheries policy

- a common system of indirect taxation, the value-added tax (VAT), and common customs duties and **excise**

- funding for research

- funding for aid to disadvantaged regions

The EU's external policy on the single market specifies:

- a common external **tariff** and a common position in international trade negotiations

- funding of programs in other Eastern European countries and developing countries

COOPERATION AREAS

EU member states cooperate in other areas as well. Member states can vote in European Parliament elections. Intelligence sharing and cooperation in criminal matters are carried out through EUROPOL and the Schengen Information System.

The EU is working to develop common foreign and security policies. Many member states are resisting such a move, however, saying these are sensitive areas best left to individual member states. Arguing in favor of a common approach to security and foreign policy are countries like France and Germany, who insist that a safer and more secure Europe can only become a reality under the EU umbrella.

One of the EU's great achievements has been to create a boundary-free area within which people, goods, services, and money can move around freely; this ease of movement is sometimes called "the four freedoms." As the EU grows in size, so do the challenges facing it—and yet its fifty-year history has amply demonstrated the power of cooperation.

EUROPEAN UNION—ESTONIA

Europe is proud of its "bright idea," a union with economic and political power.

The EU believes that it can use its power to act as a "lighthouse" for the rest of the world.

KEY EU INSTITUTIONS

Five key institutions play a specific role in the EU.

THE EUROPEAN PARLIAMENT

The European Parliament (EP) is the democratic voice of the people of Europe. Directly elected every five years, the Members of the European Parliament (MEPs) sit not in national **blocs** but in political groups representing the seven main political parties of the member states. Each group reflects the political ideology of the national parties to which its members belong. Some MEPs are not attached to any political group.

COUNCIL OF THE EUROPEAN UNION

The Council of the European Union (formerly known as the Council of Ministers) is the main leg-

islative and decision-making body in the EU. It brings together the nationally elected representatives of the member-state governments. One minister from each of the EU's member states attends council meetings. It is the forum in which government representatives can assert their interests and reach compromises. Increasingly, the Council of the European Union and the EP are acting together as colegislators in decision-making processes.

EUROPEAN COMMISSION

The European Commission does much of the day-to-day work of the EU. Politically independent, the commission represents the interests of the EU as a whole, rather than those of individual member states. It drafts proposals for new European laws, which it presents to the EP and the Council of the European Union. The European Commission makes sure EU decisions are implemented properly and supervises the way EU funds are spent. It also sees that everyone abides by the European treaties and European law.

The EU member-state governments choose the European Commission president, who is then approved by the EP. Member states, in consultation with the incoming president, nominate the other European Commission members, who must also be approved by the EP. The commission is appointed for a five-year term, but can be dismissed by the EP. Many members of its staff work in Brussels, Belgium.

COURT OF JUSTICE

Headquartered in Luxembourg, the Court of Justice of the European Communities consists of one independent judge from each EU country. This court ensures that the common rules decided in the EU are understood and followed uniformly by all the members. The Court of Justice settles disputes over how EU treaties and legislation are interpreted. If national courts are in doubt about how to apply EU rules, they must ask the Court of Justice. Individuals can also bring proceedings against EU institutions before the court.

COURT OF AUDITORS

EU funds must be used legally, economically, and for their intended purpose. The Court of Auditors, an independent EU institution located in Luxembourg, is responsible for overseeing how EU money is spent. In effect, these auditors help European taxpayers get better value for the money that has been channeled into the EU.

OTHER IMPORTANT BODIES

1. European Economic and Social Committee: expresses the opinions of organized civil society on economic and social issues

2. Committee of the Regions: expresses the opinions of regional and local authorities

3. European Central Bank: responsible for monetary policy and managing the euro

4. European Ombudsman: deals with citizens' complaints about mismanagement by any EU institution or body

5. European Investment Bank: helps achieve EU objectives by financing investment projects

Together with a number of agencies and other bodies completing the system, the EU's institutions have made it the most powerful organization in the world.

EU MEMBER STATES

In order to become a member of the EU, a country must have a stable democracy that guarantees the rule of law, human rights, and protection of minorities. It must also have a functioning market economy as well as a civil service capable of applying and managing EU laws.

The EU provides substantial financial assistance and advice to help candidate countries prepare themselves for membership. As of October 2004, the EU has twenty-five member states. Bulgaria and Romania are likely to join in 2007, which would bring the EU's total population to nearly 500 million.

In December 2004, the EU decided to open negotiations with Turkey on its proposed membership. Turkey's possible entry into the EU has been fraught with controversy. Much of this controversy has centered on Turkey's human rights record and the divided island of Cyprus. If allowed to join the EU, Turkey would be its most-populous member state.

The 2004 expansion was the EU's most ambitious enlargement to date. Never before has the EU embraced so many new countries, grown so much in terms of area and population, or encompassed so many different histories and cultures. As the EU moves forward into the twenty-first century, it will undoubtedly continue to grow in both political and economic strength.

A new day dawns for Estonia as it takes its place in the European Union.

7 ESTONIA IN THE EUROPEAN UNION

Estonia joined the EU in May 2004, making it one of the EU's newest members. Estonia was, in fact, the first Baltic country to begin negotiations for joining the EU, a process that began in 1998. The majority of Estonians were eager to become part of this organization, but there are still many Estonians who do not support EU membership and feel threatened by this new development in their

Resistance to EU Membership

Much of the resistance to EU membership can be explained by the fact that Estonia is such a newly independent nation. The country has spent the vast majority of its history under other nations' control. Now, some people see becoming part of the EU as a threat to national sovereignty. As part of the EU, Estonia is expected to abide by the laws and regulations that apply to all EU countries and faces penalties for noncompliance. For every EU member country, this does reduce a certain degree of sovereignty. For example, to be considered for EU membership, Estonia had to review its strict language laws and integration policies and make revisions to bring these laws and policies more in line with international standards. Some people don't feel their nation should have to conform to international standards regarding internal matters, but most people feel they gain more by becoming a member of the EU than they lose.

One of the things citizens of EU members gain is the ability to work in all the member states without having to apply for work permits. However, for most of the member states who were admitted in 2004, Estonia included, there are currently restrictions on this right. In order to protect other member countries from a possible flood of new workers, Estonians will only be able to work in countries, like the Netherlands, that have specifically dropped restrictions. Other countries will not allow workers without work permits for at least two years and for a possible maximum of seven years. This arrangement has some Estonians upset. They feel they should have the full rights of membership from the very beginning.

Another major reason for resistance to EU membership is the fear of brain drain—losing highly educated or skilled citizens to other countries that might offer benefits such as better jobs, pay, or, lifestyle. Brain drain is something that has affected many nations around the world as individuals move to neighboring (or even distant) countries searching for a better life for themselves and their families, and it has a serious impact on the nations they have left. Some countries now have serious shortages of important professionals like doctors, nurses, and researchers because so many have moved abroad.

Support for Membership

Despite the resistance, Estonia has become a member of the EU, and most Estonians support this new development in their history. They feel that membership has more pros

Estonia is a modern nation, but many residents still follow old folk ways.
This woman is collecting edible greens in a Tallinn city park.

Estonians hope to navigate the risks of European Union membership,
walking forward to closer integration with the developed nations of the continent.

than cons and will open great opportunities for their citizens and their country. Many people believe that, even if great numbers of Estonians choose to travel, study, or work in other parts of Europe, they will ultimately return to their homeland, bringing what they have learned and gained with them.

Another benefit of EU membership is that the entire union has an interest in keeping each individual member economically stable and growing. As part of a union, weakness in one nation can trigger weakness for all, so all nations recognize the need for cooperation to keep each other strong. This translates into many minds being pulled together and the possibility of financial and other forms of aid for countries experiencing economic problems or in need of development. Estonia began benefiting in this way even before its EU membership became official. For example, in preparation for EU membership, Estonia received financial aid and other assistance to develop areas of its rural economy. The main goals of the rural development program were to strengthen agricultural production and improve processing; create jobs in rural areas through promoting rural tourism, handicrafts, and other local economic ventures; and improving rural infrastructure through building access roads and improving water supplies, electricity grids, and telecommunications systems. These efforts began with EU financing before Estonia was granted membership and will continue now that it is part of the EU.

Estonians hope that, rather than losing the best and the brightest to other countries, Estonians will

In spring, the lilac bushes in Estonia's countryside seem to explode with fragrant blossoms.

go abroad, learn the best skills and come in contact with the brightest people other countries have to offer, and use what they've learned and the contacts they've made to improve Estonia. They also hope that EU membership will increase the rest of Europe and the world's knowledge about Estonia, its history, culture, and everything it has to offer.

A Calendar of Estonian Festivals

January: New Year's Day

February: Independence Day, commemoration of the independence declaration of 1918, is celebrated on February 24. The **Tartu Ski Marathon** is held in mid-February. The **Student Jazz Festival**, celebrated in Tallinn at mid-month, is an international event featuring musicians mostly from the Baltic countries.

March: Day of the Setu Lace, is a traditional Setu festival celebrated on the first of the month.

April: Jazzkaar, is another jazz festival held in Tallinn. **University Spring Days** is spring break for students in Tartu and an excuse to get wild.

May: May Day is celebrated May 1.

June: Võidupüha (Victory Day), celebrated on June 23, commemorates the 1919 Battle of Võnnu. June 24 is Jaanipäev (St. John's Day). **Pühajärve Beach Festival** is a music festival with local and international musicians. Also in June are **Old Tallinn Days**, a festival in the Old Town of Tallinn, and **FiESTa**, an international music and theater festival in Pärnu.

July: Õllesummer is the Baltic and Scandinavian regions' largest beer festival. **Tallinn Rock Summer** is a three-day celebration featuring rock music from around the world. Pärnu hosts the **Visual Anthropology Festival**, a cultural film festival also held in July.

August: The **Day of Restoration of Independence** is celebrated August 20. Music festivals are popular in August. They include the **International Organ Music Festival**, concerts featuring organs take place all over the country; **International Bagpipe Music Festival**; **Classical Music Festival**; and the **Country Music Festival**. At the **Day of the Setu Kingdom**, a new Setu king is appointed.

September: Lillepidu, an international flower festival, is held in Tallinn in September.

December: Jõulud (Christmas), is celebrated December 25. **Boxing Day** is celebrated the next day. **Winter Days**, celebrations held in Tallinn's Old Town, are also part of Estonia's December festivities.

Cucumber and Sour Cream Salad

Ingredients
4 medium cucumbers
1 tablespoon of coarse salt or 2 tablespoons of table salt
1/2 teaspoon of white distilled vinegar
Dressing:
3 hard-boiled eggs
1 teaspoon Dijon or Düsseldorf mustard
1/3 cup of sour cream
2 teaspoons of white wine vinegar
1/4 teaspoon of sugar
1/8 teaspoon of white pepper
4 to 6 large lettuce leaves, well washed and dried
1 tablespoon of finely cut fresh dill leaves

Directions
Peel the cucumbers, then cut in half lengthwise. Scoop out and discard the seeds. Cut cucumbers into half-inch-thick slices and place in a large mixing bowl with salt and vinegar. Stir until cucumbers are coated, and then let sit for about thirty minutes.

Meanwhile, peel the eggs, cut in half, and scoop out the yolks. Cut the whites into thin strips (about 1/8-inch wide) and set aside.

In a small bowl, mash the egg yolks with a fork or the back of a large wooden spoon until reduced to fine powder. Add the mustard, sour cream, and vinegar a little at a time, beating until the mixture is smooth. Add sugar and pepper.

Drain the cucumbers, pat them dry with paper towels. Rinse and dry the bowl. Return the cucumbers to the bowl and add the sliced egg whites.

Pour dressing over cucumber/egg mixture, and toss gently until well coated. Add salt and pepper to taste.

Place lettuce leaves on a large plate and mound the salad on top. Sprinkle the dill over the salad and chill until ready to serve.

Fried Potato Patties

Ingredients
3 pounds of potatoes
4 eggs
1/2–3/4 cup of flour
1 1/2 tablespoons of salt
6 tablespoons of butter for frying

Directions
Peel potatoes and cut into quarters. Place in large pot with enough water to completely cover all of the potatoes. Boil uncovered until a fork inserts easily. Remove from heat and drain well.

Return potatoes to the pot (but do not put over heat) or into a large bowl. Mash with a potato masher, fork, or electric mixer. Add the egg, 1/2 cup flour, and salt, and beat until the mixture is smooth and thick. If the mixture is too soft or runny, beat additional flour in one table-spoon at a time until it forms a soft dough that holds together on a spoon.

When the potato mixture is thick enough to hold together, form it into a ball and place on a heavily floured breadboard or countertop.

Shape dough into a rectangle and sprinkle more flour over top. Brush a rolling pin with flour and roll dough until the rectangle is about 1-inch thick. During the rolling process, dust the dough, rolling surface, and rolling pin with more flour any time it seems like the dough may begin to stick.

Cut the dough into diamond-shaped patties by slicing the dough into 2-inch wide strips and then slicing diagonally across those strips, mak-ing the diagonal slices 2 1/2 inches apart. Score the top of each patty with shallow lines running lengthwise.

Place a large, heavy-bottomed skillet over medium-high heat. Melt 2 tablespoons of butter and allow to bubble until foam has almost dis-appeared (do not allow the butter to burn). Fry the patties in small batches (6 to 8 at a time) for 3 to 5 minutes on each side. Begin serving immediately or place on a serving platter, cover with tin foil, and keep in a warm oven until all patties are ready to serve.

Su it
A traditional Christmas dish

Ingredients
2 pounds neck bones, cut into chunks
3 pounds pork roast, cut into chunks
1 large onion chopped
1 pound carrots, diced
5 bay leaves
15–20 pepper corns
1 teaspoon salt
1 package clear gelatin

Directions
This recipe will have to cook slowly for at least 8 hours, so it is best to start the evening before and allow the slow cooking to happen overnight.

Brush a heavy-bottomed pot with a little bit of oil and place on stovetop. Cook meat over medium heat until browned on all sides.

Transfer the browned meat to a slow cooker, and add all the other ingredients except the gelatin. Cook for at least 8 hours or until very tender.

Strain the meat, reserving the liquid but discarding the bay leaves, peppercorns, and any remaining vegetables. Pull the meat from the bones and discard bones and fat. Place the meat in a 9 x 13 inch pan or in a large mold.

In a large saucepan, bring the liquid (there should be about 4 cups) to a boil. Dissolve the gelatin according to the package directions and stir into the boiling liquid. Pour the liquid over the meat and chill until firm (this will take a couple of hours). Sprinkle white vinegar on top to serve.

PROJECT AND REPORT IDEAS

- Make one of the recipes in this book, or find another Estonian recipe. Now, research foods from other ethnic groups. Can you find a similar food from another culture? Research these food histories, looking for common origins or cultural ties. What do these foods and cultures share? What are their differences? Make both these foods and present them and your findings to your class.

- Pick an event in Estonian history or an aspect of Estonian culture that interests you. Borrow a video camera from a family member, friend, or library. Film a re-creation of this event or cultural performance. Ask your classmates to participate, and present your film in class. If you don't have access to a video camera, write a play or create a performance and present it to your class.

- Search for an Estonian family, church, or center in your community or somewhere close by. Interview members of the community about their history, culture, and how they came to be part of your community. On your own or with their help, create a scrapbook that tells their stories. Present it to your class and to your community.

- Conduct further research on the member states who were admitted to the EU in 2004. Write a report discussing these states, their similarities and differences, how EU membership will affect these countries, and how their membership might affect the EU as a whole.

- With a group of your classmates, pretend you are a country considering entry to the EU. Research what it would mean for your country to join the EU. Elect a president from your country, and then divide your remaining members into two groups, those favoring accession and those opposed. Hold a town hall meeting where the two sides will present the pros and cons of EU membership to the president. At the end of the meeting, have your president decide whether or not your country will join based on the arguments you presented.

CHRONOLOGY

1200s	German, Danish, Swedish, and Russian conquerors divide Estonia into feudal states.
late 1600s	The first Old Believers come to Estonia.
1632	Estonia's first university is established.
1710	Russian aggression brings the region under Russian control.
1721	Estonia officially becomes part of Russia; it remains so until 1918.
1775	The city of Tartu is almost destroyed by fire.
1860s–1880s	Estonians experience a period known as the Era of Enlightenment.
1906	The first professional theater begins in Estonia.
1918	Estonia declares its independence from Russia, and its War of Liberation begins.
1939	The Soviet army begins establishing military bases in Estonia.
1991	The Soviet Union disbands.
1992	Estonia holds elections.
May 2004	Estonia joins the EU.
2005	Estonia and Russia reach agreement over their land border.

Raun, Toivo U. *Estonia and the Estonians*, 2nd ed. Stanford, Calif.: Hoover Institution Press, 2001.
Spilling, Michael. *Estonia*, 2nd ed. New York: Benchmark Books, 1999.
Williams, Nicola, Debra Herrmann, and Cathryn Kemp. *Estonia, Latvia and Lithuania*, 3rd ed. Oakland, Calif.: Lonely Planet Publications, 2003.

Cultural and Historic Information
www.estonica.org

Estonia's Official State Web Center
www.riik.ee/en

Estonian Festival Listings
www.kultuuriinfo.ee

Europa: The European Union Online
europa.ee.int

European Union: Delegation of the European Commission to the USA
www.eurunion.org

Information about Estonia
www.visitestonia.com
www.cia.gov/cia/publications/factbook

Tartu Tourist Information Centre
turism.tartumaa.ee/index.php?lang=eng

EU Information
europa.eu.int

FOR MORE INFORMATION

Consulate General of Estonia
600 3rd Avenue, 26th Floor
New York, NY 10016

Estonian Embassy
260 Dalhousie Street, Suite 210
Ottawa, Ontario K1N 7E4
Tel.: 613-789-4222
e-mail: embassy.ottawa@mfa.ee

Estonian Embassy
2131 Massachusetts Avenue, NW
Washington, DC 20008
Tel.: 202-588-0101
e-mail: info@estemb.org

Estonian Tourist Board
Liivalaia 13/15
Tallinn 10118
Estonia
Tel.: 372-627-9770
Fax: 372-627-9777
e-mail: tourism@eas.ee

U.S. Department of State
2201 C Street NW
Washington, DC 20520
Tel.: 202-647-4000

advocated: Spoke in favor of something.

appease: To pacify someone.

archaeological: Relating to archaeology, the scientific study of ancient cultures through the examination of their material remains.

autonomous: Able to act independently.

biodiversity: The range of organisms present in a given ecological community or system.

blocs: United groups of countries.

capital: Wealth in the form of money or property.

catalyzing: Causing a particular thing to happen.

collectivized: Organized or ran something according to the principles of collective control.

communist: Someone supporting the political theory or system in which all property and wealth is owned in a classless society by all members of a community.

coup: The sudden overthrow of a government and seizure of political power, usually in a violent way.

Crusades: Military expeditions made by European Christians during the eleventh through thirteenth centuries to retake areas captured by Muslim forces.

decimated: Inflicted so much damage on something that it is nearly destroyed or beyond repair.

excise: A tax on goods used domestically.

exploitation: Unfair treatment or use of someone or something, usually for personal gain.

feudal: Relating to the legal and social system of medieval Europe, in which vassals held land from lords in exchange for military service.

impeccably: Done so flawlessly to be beyond criticism.

invertebrates: Animals that do not have a backbone.

lichen: A gray, green, or yellow plant appearing in flat patches on rocks and other surfaces that is a combination of fungi and algae growing together.

nation-state: An independent state recognized by and able to interact with other states.

pagan: A religion that is not one of the world's main religions and regarded as questionable.

peat: A compacted deposit of partially decomposed organic debris, usually saturated with water.

perpetuating: Making something continue, usually for a long time.

ratified: Officially approved.

serfdom: The condition of being an agricultural worker, especially in feudal Europe, who worked the land belonging to the landowner and was bought and sold with the land.

solidarity: The act of standing together, presenting a united front.

stagnancy: A period of inactivity.

supplant: To take the place of something else.

sustainability: The ability to be maintained in an ecological balance.

tariff: A government tax levied on goods, usually imports.

tsar: An emperor of Russia before 1917.

urbanization: The act of making an area of countryside or villages into a town or part of one.

vascular: Tissue specialized for conducting sap.

watershed: The land area that drains into a particular lake, river, or ocean.

INDEX

Picture Credits

All photos are by Benjamin Stewart, with the following exceptions:

Used with permission of the European Communities: pp. 54–55, 57, 60, 63, 64

Photos.com: pp. 58, 66

BIOGRAPHIES

AUTHOR

Autumn Libal is a freelance author and illustrator living in Toronto, Canada. She received her degree from Smith College and has written numerous educational books and articles for children ranging on topics from cultural issues to teen health concerns. Other Mason Crest series she has written for include WOMEN'S ISSUES: GLOBAL TRENDS, HISPANIC HERITAGE, and NORTH AMERICAN INDIANS TODAY.

SERIES CONSULTANT

Ambassador John Bruton served as Irish Prime Minister from 1994 until 1997. As prime minister, he helped turn Ireland's economy into one of the fastest-growing in the world. He was also involved in the Northern Ireland Peace Process, which led to the 1998 Good Friday Agreement. During his tenure as Ireland's prime minister, he also presided over the European Union presidency in 1996 and helped finalize the Stability and Growth Pact, which governs management of the euro. Before being named the European Commission Head of Delegation in the United States, he was a member of the convention that drafted the European Constitution, signed October 29, 2004.

The European Commission Delegation to the United States represents the interests of the European Union as a whole, much as ambassadors represent their countries' interests to the U.S. government. Matters coming under European Commission authority are negotiated between the commission and the U.S. administration.